God Keeps His Promises

by Ruth Shannon Odor

illustrated by Andra Chase

The Standard Publishing Company, Cincinnati, Ohio
A division of Standex International Corporation
©1992 by The Standard Publishing Company

All rights reserved.

Printed in the United States of America
99 98 97 96 95 94 93 92   5 4 3 2 1
Library of Congress Catalog Card Number 91-67212
ISBN 0-87403-931-2

**G**od took care of Noah and his family and the animals during the flood.

God made a promise to Noah.
Do you know what it was?

TURN THE PAGE ▶▶▶

AND SEE

God said that there will always be spring.
There will always be summer.
There will always be fall.
There will always be winter.
As long as the earth lasts, there will
always be seasons.
God is still keeping His promise.

N oah and his family and the animals were
happy to be out of the ark.
Noah thanked God for taking care of them.
God made another promise to Noah.
Do you know what it was?

TURN THE PAGE ▶▶▶

AND SEE

God said He would never again send another
flood to destroy the earth.
Then God put the very first rainbow in the
sky.
Whenever we see a rainbow, we remember
that God is keeping His promise.

God told Abraham to go to a new land.
Abraham obeyed God.
God made a promise to Abraham.
Do you know what it was?

TURN THE PAGE ▶▶▶

AND SEE

God promised Abraham and Sarah a son.
And even when they were very old, God sent
them a baby boy.
They named him Isaac.
God keeps His promises.

O ne night Jacob dreamed that he saw a ladder
that reached from earth to Heaven.
Angels were going up and down the ladder.
God spoke to Jacob that night.
He made a promise to Jacob.
Do you know what it was?

TURN THE PAGE ▶▶▶

AND SEE

God told Jacob that He would be with him.
He said that Jacob would have many children.
Soon they would be a great nation.

Jacob had twelve sons, and their children
made the nation of Israel.
God keeps His promises.

**M**oses and the people of Israel lived in the land
of Egypt.
They were slaves there.

One day God spoke to Moses from a burning bush.
God made a promise to him.
Do you know what it was?

TURN THE PAGE ▶▶▶

AND SEE

God promised Moses that He would lead His
   people out of Egypt.
He would give them a new land of their own.
And God did.
He led the people out of the land of Egypt.
He gave them the land of Canaan.
God keeps His promises.

Gideon was hiding from the Midianite soldiers
    as he threshed wheat.
Suddenly an angel stood before Gideon.
The angel told him a promise from God.
Do you know what it was?

TURN THE PAGE ▶▶▶

AND SEE

God promised to help Gideon drive the Midianites away. He told Gideon exactly what to do. One night Gideon's men went to the Midianite camp.

They blew trumpets, broke jars, raised torches,
and shouted. The Midianite soldiers ran away!
God keeps His promises.

David was a shepherd boy who lived in
Bethlehem.
When he was a man, he became the king.

One day God's prophet Nathan told King David a
   promise from God.
Do you know what it was?

TURN THE PAGE ▶▶▶

AND SEE

God promised David that he could make plans to
    build God's house—the beautiful temple.
But his son Solomon would actually build it.
As planned, Solomon had the beautiful temple built.
It stood on a high hill in Jerusalem—a place for
    God's people to go and worship.
God keeps His promises.

God made a promise to His people.
It was the most important promise of all.
It was for you and me too.
God told the promise to His prophets.
Do you know what it was?

TURN THE PAGE ▶▶▶

AND SEE

God said, "I will send my Son to earth.
He will be born in Bethlehem.
He will be the Savior."

God sent Jesus to earth.
He was born in Bethlehem.
He grew to be a man.
He died for us because He loves us.
Who is Jesus?

TURN THE PAGE ▶▶▶

AND SEE

Jesus is our Savior.
He arose from the dead just as He
    said He would.
God keeps His promises.

Paul traveled to many places to tell people
   about Jesus.
Once Paul was on a very dangerous journey.
While he was asleep, God spoke to him.
God made a promise.
Do you know what it was?

TURN THE PAGE ▶▶▶

AND SEE

God promised to keep Paul and all those with him safe during a terrible storm and shipwreck.

And God did.

The ship was wrecked, but Paul and the others were able to get safely to land.

God keeps His promises.

God made another promise.
It is for you and me.
It is a promise about Jesus.
Do you know what it is?

TURN THE PAGE ▶▶▶

AND SEE

God has promised that someday Jesus will
    come back again.
No one except God knows when He will come.
But He will come, and everyone will see Him.
Jesus is coming again.
God keeps His promises.